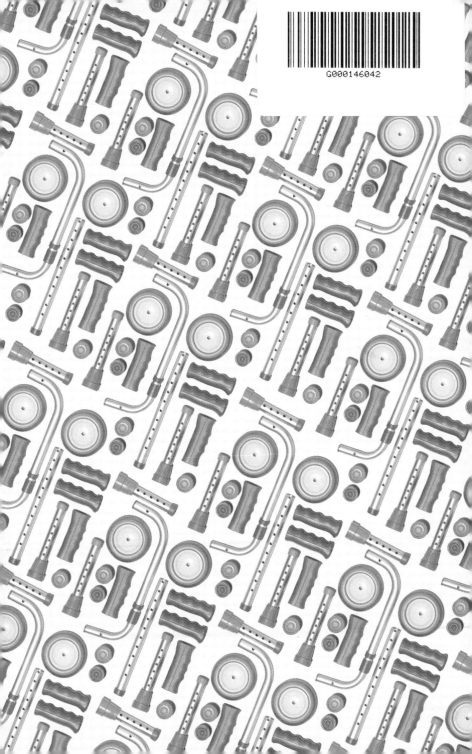

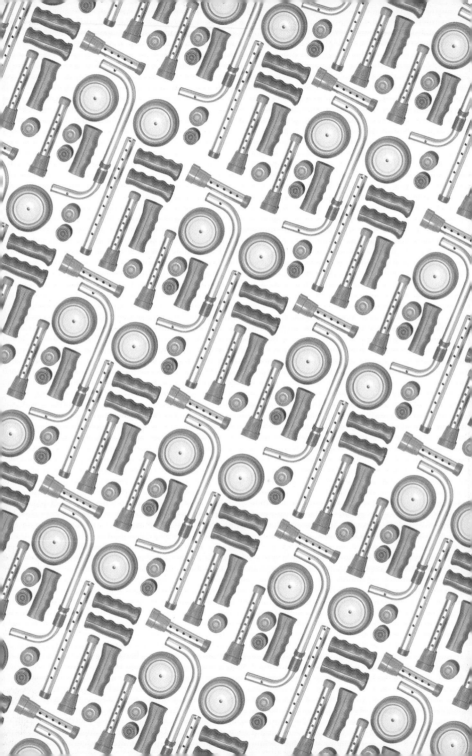

I ♥ MY ZIMMER

BY
BILL FALLOVER

PHOTOGRAPHY BY
TONY HIGGINS

sphere

SPHERE

First published in Great Britain in 2008 by Sphere
Original edition published in 2007 by Falloverart Publishing

A CIP catalogue record for this book is
available from the British Library.

ISBN 978-1-84744-256-7

Printed and bound in Italy by LEGO Spa

Sphere
An imprint of
Little, Brown Book Group
100 Victoria Embankment
London EC4Y 0DY

An Hachette Livre UK Company
www.hachettelivre.co.uk

www.littlebrown.co.uk

THE HUMBLE ZIMMER

Dear Reader

It seems like everything can be custom made these days to suit our individual tastes and needs. So why not the trusty Zimmer frame? Let's face it, if you haven't got one yet, it's only a matter of time…

In the meantime, why not take inspiration from the collection of Zimmers I have created especially for these pages? From the ancient to the artistic to the frankly terrifying, I'm sure at least one or two will take your fancy.

And so what if a couple of them wouldn't pass a Health and Safety test? Surely by our age we've earned the right to live dangerously. Caution is for the young. Half the time us old ones don't know where we are, where we're going, who we are meant to be seeing and why. Now that's dangerous!

I hope you enjoy these Zimmers as much as I've enjoyed designing and making them. Oh, and one final thing. Yes, that really is my real name.

Best wishes Bill Fallover

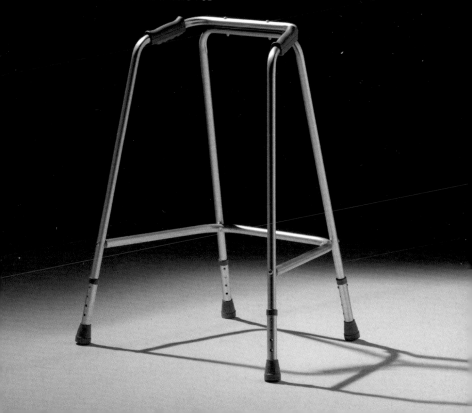

THE
FETISH ZIMMER
If you're into leather - work it out yourself!

WARNING
Good Luck!!

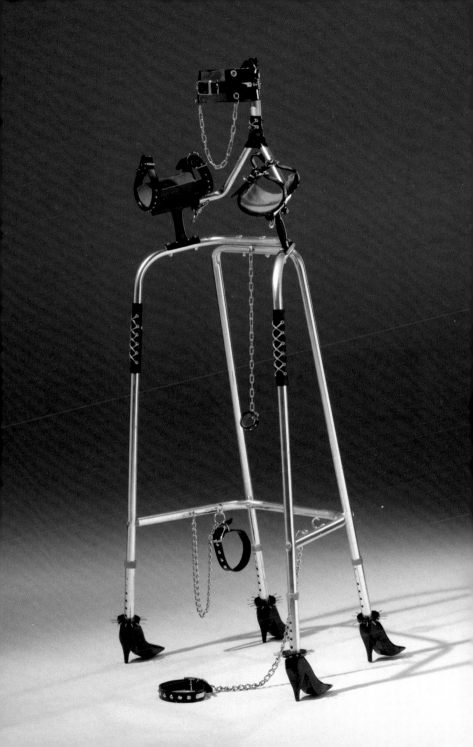

WARNING!
Do NOT let drunks
hang on for support.
Disastrous for you
and your drinks!

BAR ZIMMER

BAR ZIMMER

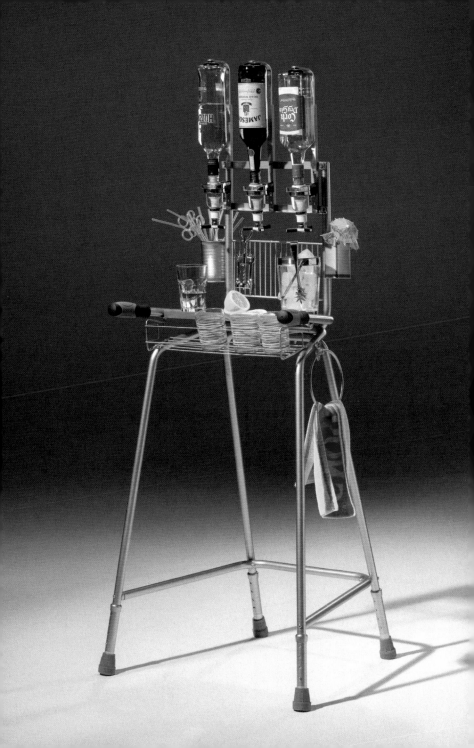

This Hedge Zimmer is accurate to within 50mm. No excuse now!

THE BEACH ZIMMER

Stick into the sand to make the perfect windbreak.
Also works well as a changing room.
Unless someone walks behind you, of course.

ALL YOU NEED IS LOVE!

THE ECO ZIMMER

Win brownie points when visiting the recycling centre.

Warning!
Keep away from naked flames – and naked bodies, if
you want to avoid splinters…

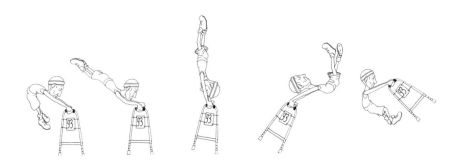

THE OLYMPIC ZIMMER

Have you lived life to the full? Have you got nothing to lose?
Golf lost its thrill?

ZIMMERTRON is the ultimate sport (for the over 70s).

Rules: The competitor must flip his or her body up and over the Zimmer. The motion of their body allows them to spin back to the ground and continue for several metres, or until their hip gives out. The winner is the last one to call for emergency medical support.

And now – look out for **ZIMMERTRON PLUS**: raced over the same distance, except that the track is on fire!

Warning: entrants should not use the Eco Zimmer.

THE DIY ZIMMER

The DIY Zimmer is
guaranteed sturdy
 for up to thirty extendable
metres.
Now with added
 'sure grip' stabilizers,
chimney grip
 and altitude pills!

ACCESSORIES

Gutter Cleaning Kit
Diving Board (for pool side only)
Window Cleaning Kit
Roof Ladder
Cat Rescue Hook

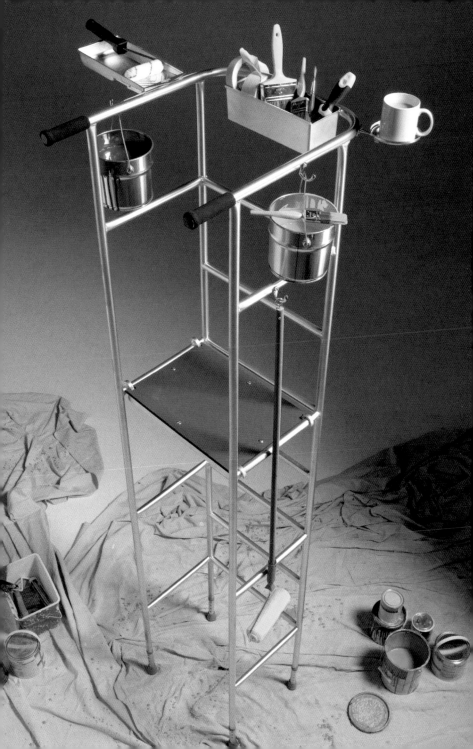

THE HITCH HIKE ZIMMER

Comes with a free set of destination letters and signs including 'To the Tea Shop', 'To Marks & Spencer' and 'Where am I?'.

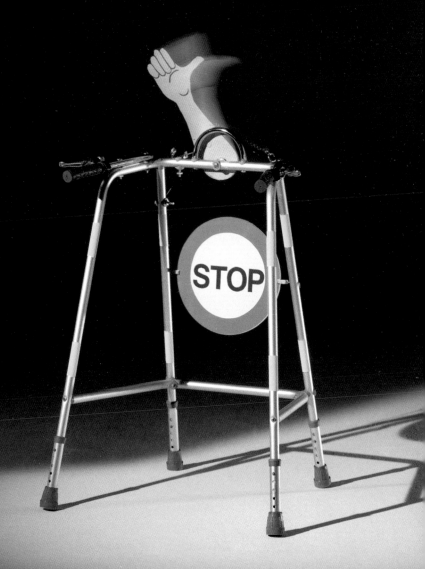

THE PARK-KEEPER ZIMMER
Does the job of four!
End spikes also offer
great protection from
cider-drinking yobs.

THE SHOWER ZIMMER

The foot-activated temperature control
means you'll never get scalded.

Instructions: Hang on for dear life

Optional hot air blower and shower curtain
for the modest bather.

THE TWITCHER ZIMMER

Wonderful for creeping up on those birds! Also a perfect guard against nagging wives – simply creep to the end of the garden and hide in the shrubbery.

Note: if wife 'accidentally' tips you and camouflaged Zimmer into the compost in process, please don't blame me.

BBQ ZIMMER

If your friends have their bar Zimmers with them, the wild party can begin!

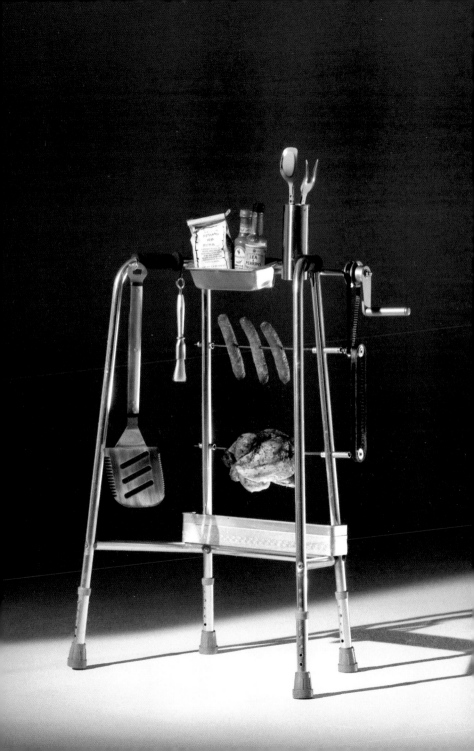

THE SUPPORTER ZIMMER

Strong enough for any size of supporter. Can be ordered in
any team colour. Due to its special platform,
gives extra viewing advantage.

Warning: may annoy people sitting in the seats behind.
Be ready with your airhorn – then they can learn what it's
like to go deaf, too.

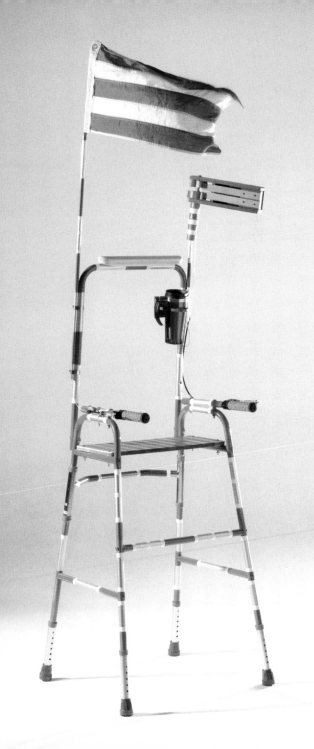

Superb for jumping pension queues.

WARNING: Avoid use on escalators, farm yards or beaches!

THE FISHING ZIMMER
What more could an old man want! Perhaps some friends with a Bar Zimmer.

OFF ROAD ZIMMER

This macho Off Road Zimmer is essential for pulling up
your old mates.
A solar-powered winch means no fuel or maintenance required.

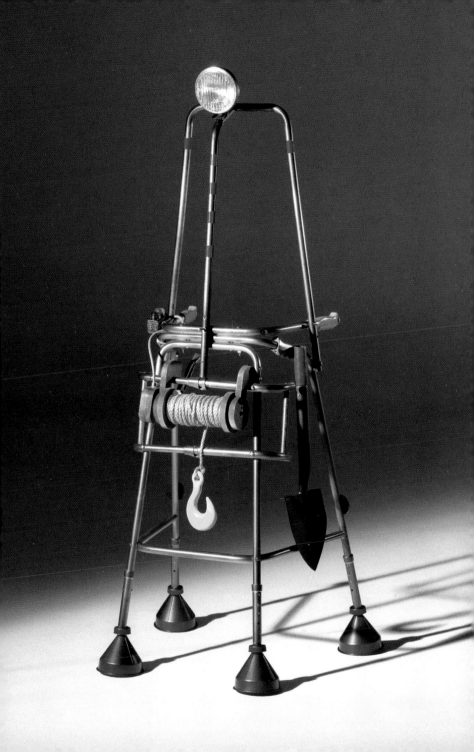

THE DANCE ZIMMER

Re-live those wild disco nights
or sedate afternoon tea dances.
The Zimmer Moves booklet is
available with each purchase.

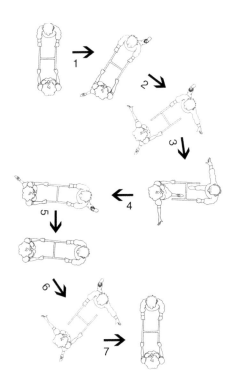

THE RECYCLE ZIMMER

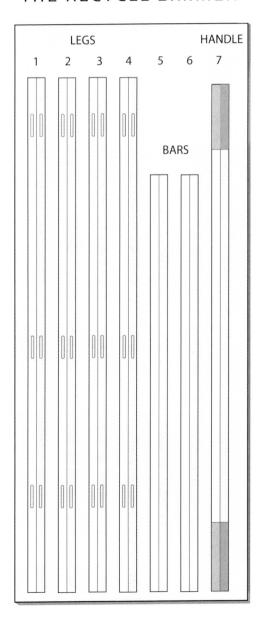

THE SAFETY ZIMMER

Us old folks have survived seventy or more years - bankruptcy, hunger, divorces, wars, lovers and all the rest. We're ultimate survivors. So, Health and Safety - up yours!.

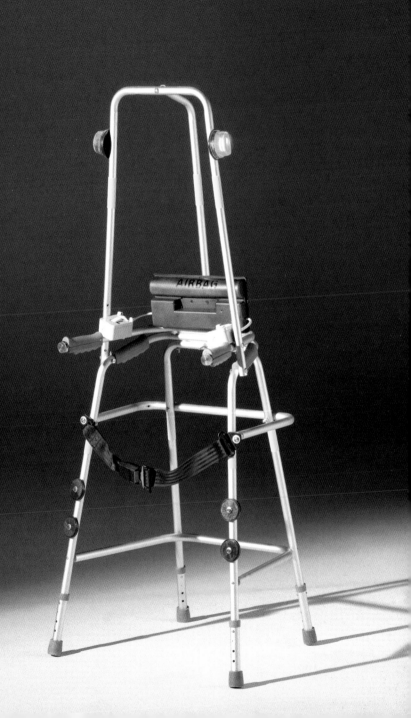

THE
CLOWN ZIMMER

Just seven balloons,
two minutes
and hey-presto!

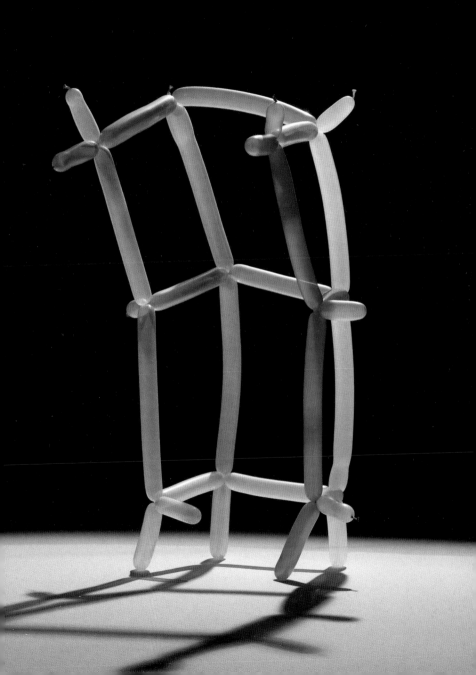

THE PUB ZIMMER

When it's time to leave the bar, or get
thrown out, flick open your Zimmer.
The satellite tracking automatically
springs into life. Programmed to your
home, the green light keeps you on track.
Keep your fish and chips safe for the
stagger home in their special holder.

Shuffle on to the next page and see
how neat it is!

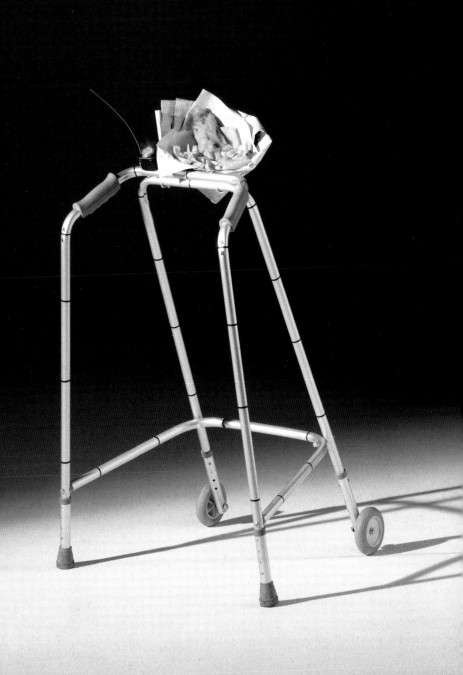

THE ASBO ZIMMER

ASBO (anti social behavior order)
AG (annoying grandchildren)

Helps keep your old folks from wandering off.

WARNING: The anti-tampering device
ensures that any attempted escape will result
in the frame springing shut, crushing its
occupant! Fun for all the family.

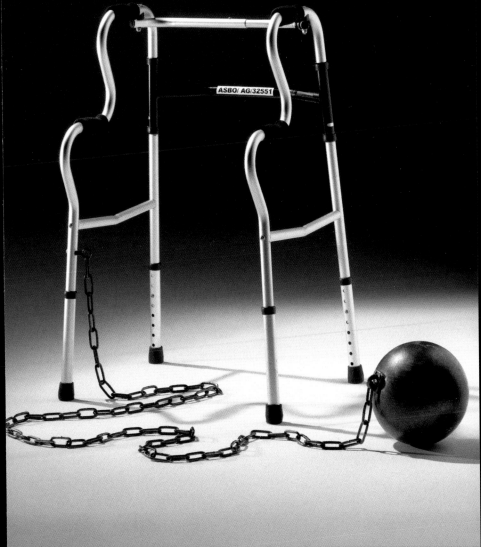

CARNIVAL ZIMMER

BE PART OF THE PARADE!

THE PIRATE ZIMMER

Standard Zimmer comes with a clip-on treasure chest,
pillage pouch, gunpowder keg, ropes and pistol holder.
The deluxe 'camp' model has a neat little compass!

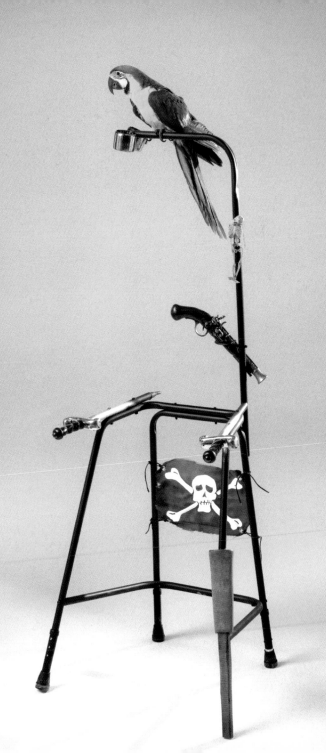

THE BOWL A ZIMMER

Approved by the O.B.A.
(Old Bowlers Association),
the Bowl A Zimmer greatly
improves your game.
No need for a mat!
Includes laser guidance.

THE CHOPPER ZIMMER

Stay young and daring!
The ultra cool Chopper Zimmer
has real pavement cred.

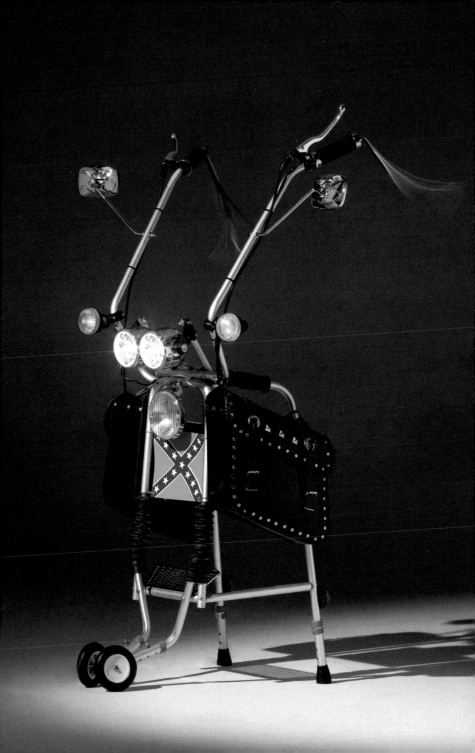

HISTORICAL ZIMMERS

Not many folks realise that the Zimmer frame is thousands of years old. Recent archaeological discoveries date the Zimmer way back to paleolithic times. The next few pages show how the Zimmer has evolved alongside its shuffling owners…

THE EGYPTIAN ZIMMER

This mummified Zimmer was found by Howard Carter shortly before he discovered the tomb of Tutankhamen. Egyptians believed that older, less mobile pharaohs would still need the support of their Zimmer in the afterlife. Local legend suggested that anyone who removed the Zimmer from its resting place would be cursed for ever. Mysteriously, Howard Carter was said to have been plagued with achy hip joints for the rest of his days...

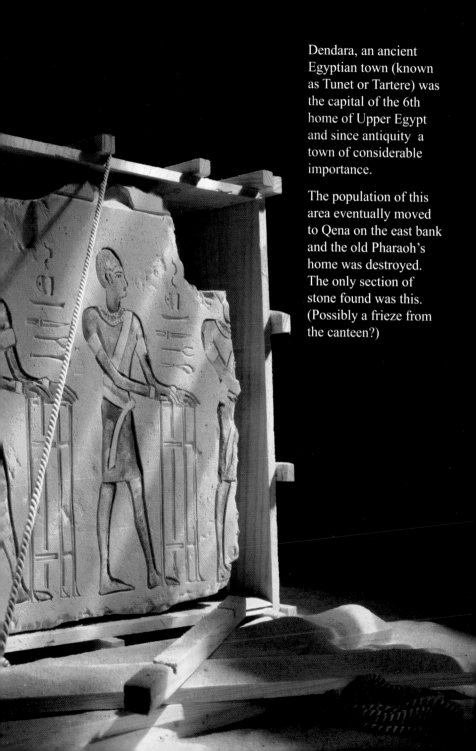

Dendara, an ancient Egyptian town (known as Tunet or Tartere) was the capital of the 6th home of Upper Egypt and since antiquity a town of considerable importance.

The population of this area eventually moved to Qena on the east bank and the old Pharaoh's home was destroyed. The only section of stone found was this. (Possibly a frieze from the canteen?)

THE INCA ZIMMER

One flame on the Inca Zimmer represents ten years of life, proving the Incas live well into their 70s. Masters of goldcraft, the Incas fashioned the golden knobs to represent their most precious commodity, the potato! It didn't take long for the western world to latch on to this delicacy from Peru.

**THE
VICTORIAN ZIMMER**

Legs had to be covered
in Victorian times!

WARNING!
To avoid being arrested keep
away from high winds.

THE CAVE ZIMMER

Period of the Roundheaded men, Africa.
Probably later than the early neolithic period.
This painting proves that the Roundheaded men
were nagged by their women.

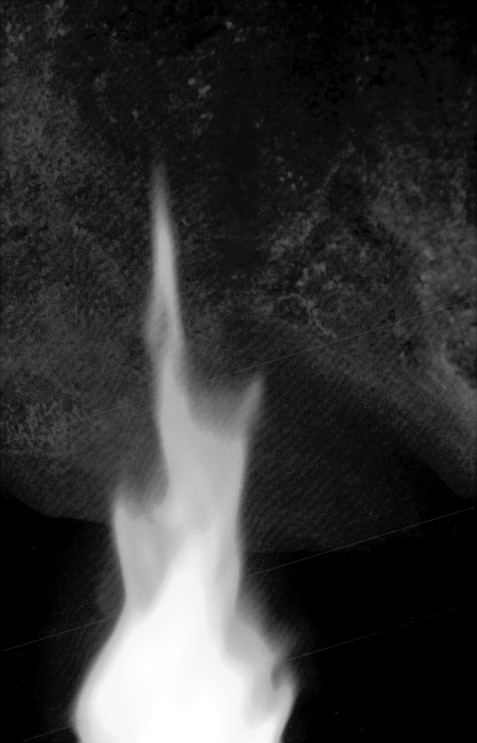

You had to be fit to use the Stone Age Zimmer.
We can only imagine the rejoicing when the
Bronze Age began.

THE ROMAN ZIMMER

Zimmus Maximus was the oldest legion in the Roman army. After retirement they spent most of their time down the pub playing darts. Their accuracy became legendary.

THE CELTIC ZIMMER

Renowned for their iron work and craftsmanship, the
Celts took pride in showing off their wealth while
honouring the importance of the pint!

THE CHINESE ZIMMER

The artist 'T'ang Chou' from the Kiangsi province created the now world-famous willow pattern while living in an old people's home on the banks of a river.

A small selection of Art Zimmers

THE
POP ART
ZIMMER

THE CUBIST ZIMMER

INFLUENCED BY MARCEL DUCHAMP

THE SURREALIST ZIMMER

Influenced by Magritte

THE
ABSTRACT
ZIMMER

Not to 'everybody's' taste.

A small selection of rejected Zimmers

Not a healthy option for gardens (too many rose bushes).
Could act as a life saver for old folks who fall into rivers.

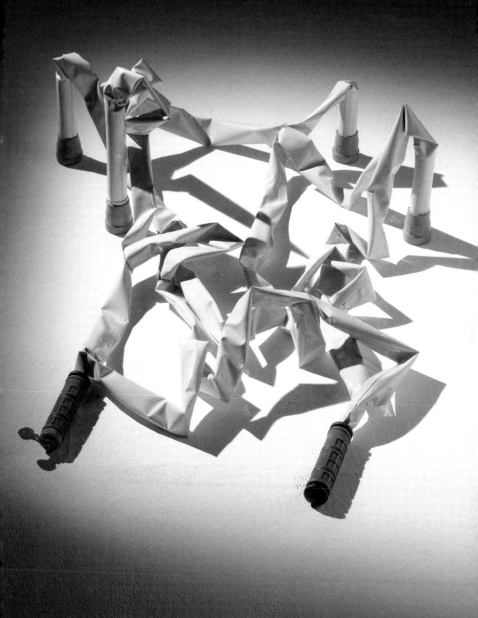

WATER SKI ZIMMER

Worked fantastically well over jumps until speed exceeded 55 knots!

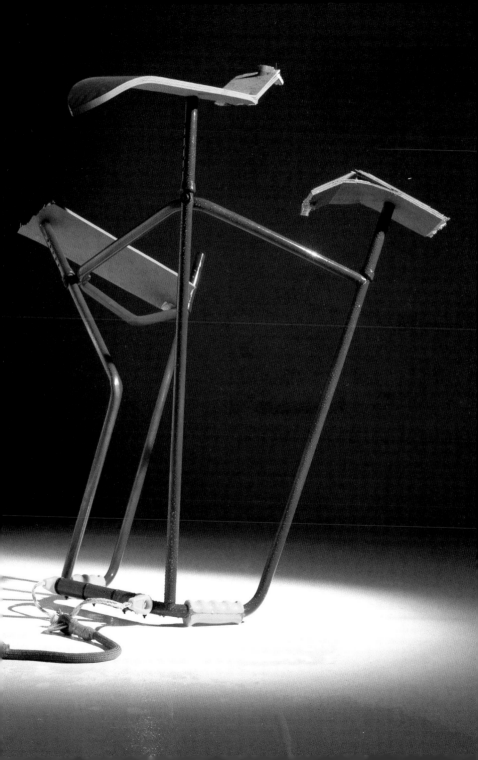

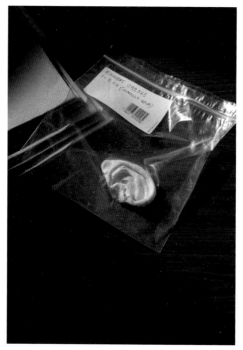

THE HAIRDRESSING ZIMMER

Not accurate enough - expensive in court!

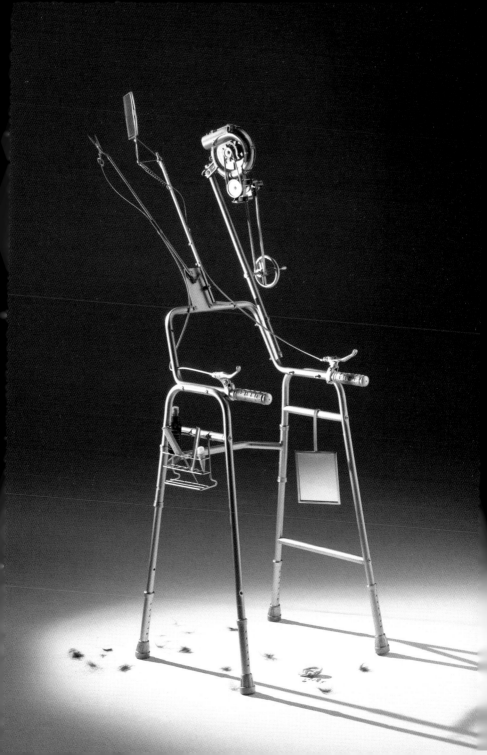

SNOW PLOUGH ZIMMER

Worked well for the first ten metres, but due to severe weather changes and slower speeds the operator quickly succumbed to hypothermia.

REJECT

THE BUNGEE ZIMMER

REJECT

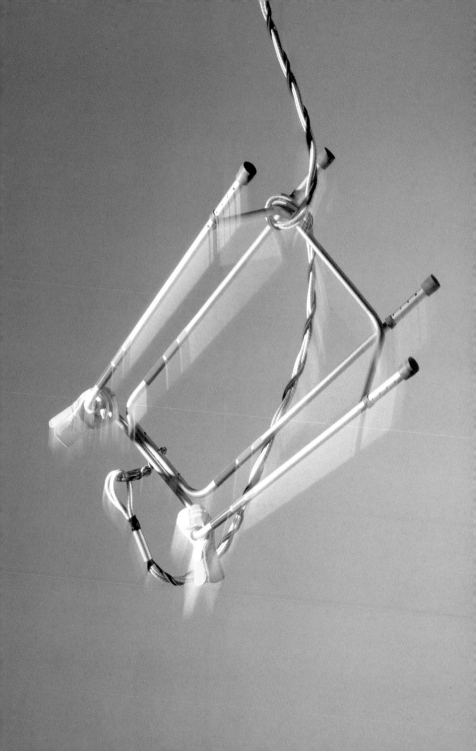

THE MINE–SWEEPING ZIMMER!

THE EDIBLE ZIMMER
Great idea for hungry folk - getting home was the problem!

BILL FALLOVER

Born in London in 1946, Bill Fallover studied art and graphic design at Hornsey College of Art. On graduating, he worked in advertising and magazine publishing, and became an award-winning designer. He later became a book and illustration designer for Penguin and Marshall Cavendish books. In 1973 he started making models for photographers and TV commercials, and later became an award-winning film production designer for TV and film, creating many special effects models. Throughout his career he has also lectured on art and design in places as diverse as Cardiff and San Francisco.

Bill Fallover has lived in Ireland for the past nineteen years with his wife and family.

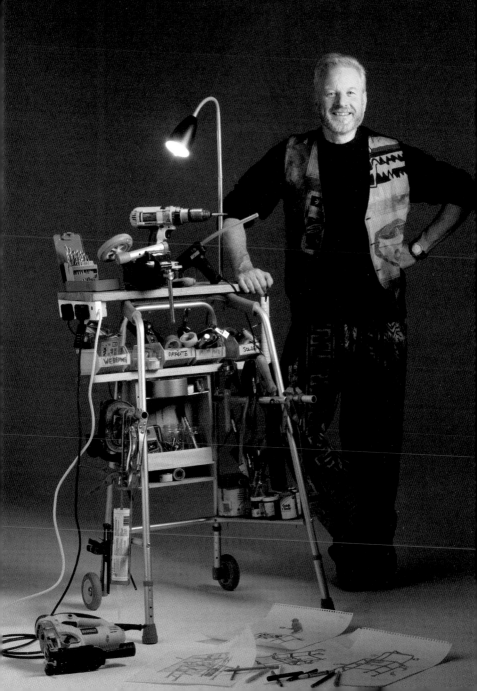

TONY HIGGINS

Born in Ireland in 1940, Tony trained as a carpenter
from the age of 14 and worked on Dublin's
Famous Liberty Hall. He spent his wages on
photographic equipment and moved into photography
in 1962, working for Con Conner on St. Stephens Green.
In 1967 Tony opened his own studio and today works
from his studio in Portobello, Dublin, shooting
advertising and fashion photography.

TIBERIU COROLIUC

Born in Romania in 1972, Tiberiu studied sociology
and had a career in marketing and advertising
before moving to Dublin. He started working
with Tony Higgins in 2003. Tiberiu believed in
digital photography from the beginning and
was invaluable in producing this book.
Tiberiu is now a fashion and advertising
photographer in Dublin.

THE PHOTO ZIMMER

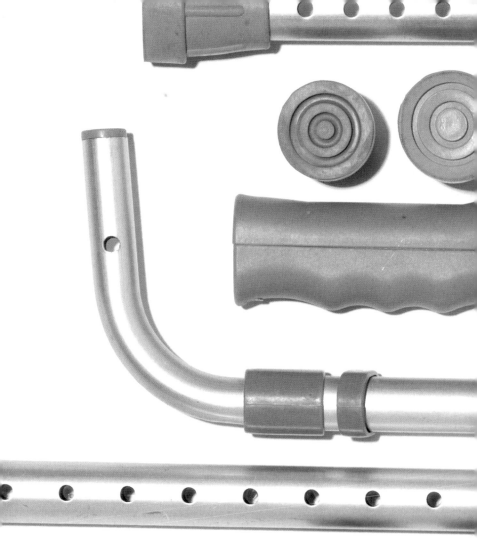

MANY THANKS

To Annie, for putting up with Zimmers all over
the house; to Joe and Harrie Fallover for their
artworks; to Mick Humby for lending me his balls;
Larry Burne for his pumps; Jimmy White for
his Zimmers; Warren Geller for his help; Eamon
Conlon for lighting up my cover

ABOUT THE NAME 'ZIMMER'

'Zimmer' is a trademark of Zimmer, Inc. However, not many people know that what we know as 'the Zimmer' was not developed or ever sold by Zimmer themselves . . .

In the 1930s, Justin O. Zimmer, the company's founder, sent another American to Britain to establish a distribution outlet for Zimmer's products. The two eventually parted ways, but Mr Zimmer's emissary managed to retain rights to the Zimmer name. While Zimmer, Inc. has long since regained use of its founder's name in the UK, in the intervening years the Zimmer frame was developed by that former distributor's company, and gained an identity of its own. So ironically, while many of Zimmer, Inc's own products are particularly useful in aiding and restoring mobility, the Zimmer frame itself is not and has not been part of its own portfolio, although Zimmer owns the Zimmer name.

Today, Zimmer, Inc. is a worldwide leader in joint replacement solutions for knee pain and hip pain, and providing comprehensive spine care solutions for acute and chronic back pain. The company also provides a broad range of trauma, dental implant, and orthopaedic surgical products. Founded in 1927, Zimmer is committed to providing effective techniques in hip replacement and knee replacement for orthopaedic surgeons who restore mobility and relieve the pain of osteoarthritis and traumatic injuries. Zimmer's minimally invasive hip and minimally invasive knee replacement systems and its wide range of related products and services make Zimmer a valuable partner to health-care providers in more than 80 countries.

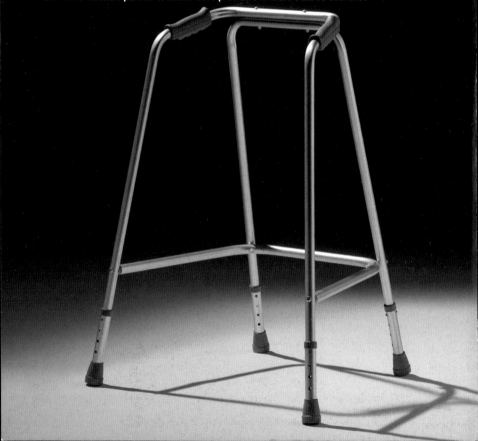

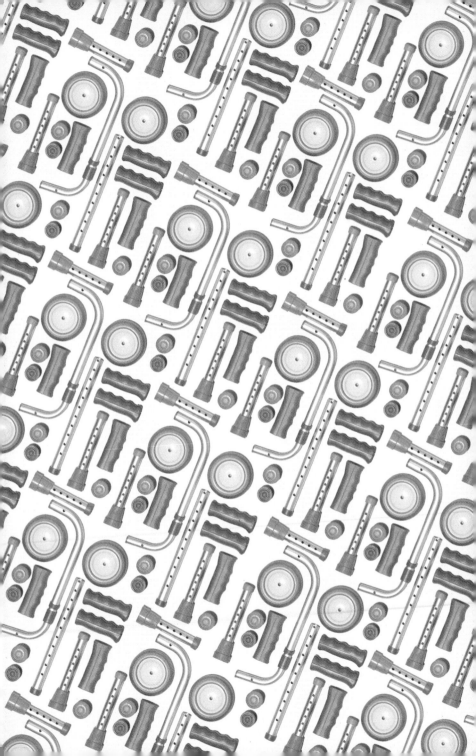

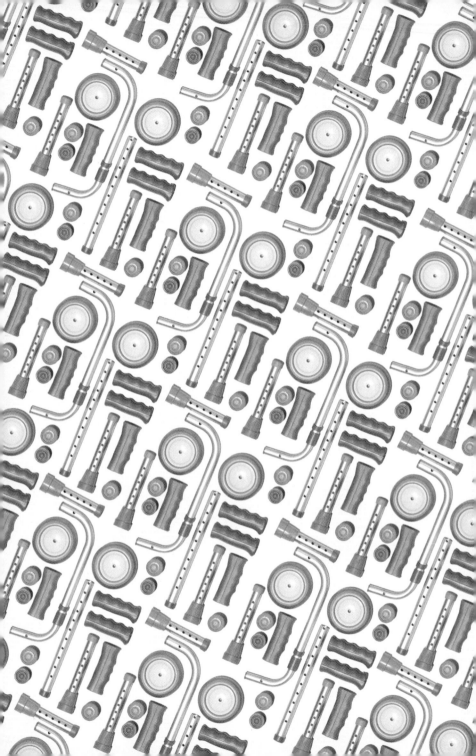